THE BIG QUAKE

CANTERBURY, SEPTEMBER 4, 2010

THE PRESS

— Proceeds from this book go
to the Red Cross Canterbury
Earthquake Appeal —

RANDOM HOUSE
NEW ZEALAND

CONTENTS

Tremors demolished buildings on Manchester Street by the entrance to Sol Square via Struthers Lane in the central city. Photo: Iain McGregor

Foreword

AT 4.35AM SEPTEMBER 4 on a balmy Christchurch Saturday, a horrific earthquake changed lives and the landscape in our city and region. The quake came without warning, and left in its wake damage never previously experienced in our city.

It's a miracle that no lives were lost as a direct result of the event. A few hours earlier, later or on another day and the scenario could have been so different. More than 1000 aftershocks have followed to further test the resilience of our residents and the thousands of people working around the clock to repair the damage. Everyone in this city has lost

something — from homes and businesses to precious personal items. And we are tired; weeks of trauma and sleepless nights take their toll.

But from all the devastation what has emerged is a wonderful sense of community spirit. Friendships have been forged. In every little nook of this city there are heroes who have pitched in to help those who have suffered. What has been reinforced is that at a time of crisis your neighbour is your most valuable ally.

Where do you begin to say thank you? Civil Defence along with our emergency services —

Prime Minister John Key, right, visited Christchurch after the 7.1 magnitude earthquake on Saturday, September 4. Mayor Bob Parker, left, took him on a tour of the city which was punctuated by a fire breaking out in a building on Worcester Street. The tour party watches the fire. Photo: Dean Kozanic

police, fire, ambulance and the Defence Force — responded above and beyond the call of duty. Thousands of volunteers took their own initiative to help. The hundreds of young people from the University of Canterbury, Lincoln University and our schools, who came together to help on the frontline further reinforced to me that the future of our city is in safe hands. Our business community from day one started planning to get our city back to normal. Media from at home and around the world worked with us to keep our residents informed. And now that we are looking to rebuild the city they are further

supporting with fundraising efforts.

Messages of support have come in from around our country and abroad. And with this have come offers to help. Millions of dollars for those who have suffered most are already pledged to the Canterbury Earthquake Appeal operated by the New Zealand Red Cross. With this, and the help of other social agencies, the business community and our people, we will rebuild our city together.

Bob Parker
Mayor of Christchurch

Preface

JOURNALISTS TRY TO LIVE by the rule of objectivity — that we are observers, a step back from events and the arguments that surround them, so that we might act as detached scrutineers of society.

The Canterbury earthquake made a mockery of that human presumption. Every one of us was part of the disaster, with our own emotions, stress, and stories.

The response of *The Press* newsroom, and our colleagues throughout the company who make our work possible, was extraordinary in its commitment to keeping our community informed — of the fear, the loss, the basic information to help us cope, the future, and of the messages of concern and support that came to us from around the world.

We would like to show what happened on September 4, 2010, and in the days afterwards. We would like to tell the stories that we found, in words, images and video.

And we would like to say how proud we are of our home and the people who live here.

ANDREW HOLDEN
Editor, The Press

Opposite page: The awning of Churchills Tavern, Colombo Street. Photo: Carys Monteath

The corner of Manchester and Worcester streets the morning of the quake. Photo: Iain McGregor

The Quake

AT 4.35 ON SATURDAY, SEPTEMBER 4, 2010, a jolt with a force that set the bells ringing in Christ Church Cathedral's tower hit Canterbury. The tremor lasted for a terrifying 30 seconds. The damage was horrendous with a huge impact on homes and property and the loss of several historic landmarks. While lives were not lost, the quake has crippled the city and some suburbs.

Centred near Darfield, about 40 kilometres west of Christchurch, the quake measured 7.1 on the Richter scale and caused the most structural damage to a New Zealand region since the 1931 Hawke's Bay earthquake.

Miraculously, in all of this, no one was killed. However, two men were seriously injured, one by a falling chimney and the other when bricks and mortar fell on his taxi in Manchester Street.

Luckily, the timing of the quake prevented fatalities. At such a late hour, few people were out in the streets, even in the central city, and people were not cooking, which prevented fires breaking out. Although power was lost to more than half of the city, cell towers ran on emergency battery power, supplying coverage to cellphones in the region, and families were able to contact each other quickly.

Massive disruption was suffered, including widespread power outages, water supplies cut off, water contamination, sewage-disposal problems, business destruction and dangerous housing. In less than a minute, a modern, relatively prosperous city was suddenly experiencing scenes reminiscent of a Third World disaster: City streets strewn with rubble, sand and water bubbling up through suburban lawns, chimneys collapsed through roofs and flooded and broken roads.

Aftershocks, ranging up to 5.4 in magnitude, kept residents on edge for several weeks. This is the story of the quake.

> ## "When the shaking woke us, I thought, 'this is it, the Alpine Fault is finally going'."
>
> — *Crile, Lyttelton*

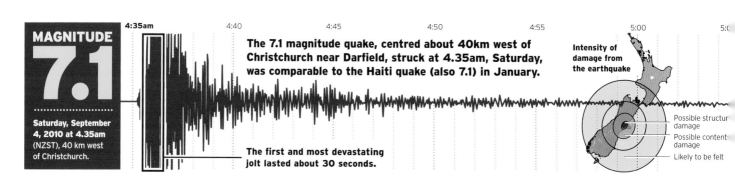

MAGNITUDE 7.1

Saturday, September 4, 2010 at 4.35am (NZST), 40 km west of Christchurch.

The 7.1 magnitude quake, centred about 40km west of Christchurch near Darfield, struck at 4.35am, Saturday, was comparable to the Haiti quake (also 7.1) in January.

The first and most devastating jolt lasted about 30 seconds.

Intensity of damage from the earthquake

Possible structur damage
Possible content damage
Likely to be felt

Opposite page: Angus Donaldson Printers at dawn, Colombo Street, Sydenham. Photo: Iain McGregor

This page top left: The damaged Repertory Theatre on Kilmore Street, which was due to be restored. Photo: Iain McGregor **Right:** The clock tower on Victoria Street stopped at the time of the earthquake (it was fast). Photo: Iain McGregor **Bottom:** The clock tower on the old Moorhouse Avenue railway station, now Science Alive, also stopped at the time of the earthquake.

Opposite page top: Shaken and curious crowds at the corner of Manchester and Worcester streets the morning of the quake. Photo: Beck Eleven **Bottom:** Extensive damage was done to both shelving and books at Canterbury University central library during the quake. Photo: Stacy Squires

Damage to shops at the corner of Edgeware Road and Barbadoes Street. Photo: Iain McGregor

Looking east along Lichfield Street the morning of the quake. Photo: Carys Monteath

Top: This house on Avonside Drive was lifted off its foundations. Photo: Iain McGregor **Bottom:** Damage to the road outside the Kaiapoi Fire Station.
Photo: Kirk Hargreaves

Top: The Kaiapoi railway line near Woodford Glen. Photo supplied by Leanne Matthews and John Overend **Bottom:** Concerned for his electorate, Clayton Cosgrove visits a house in Kaiapoi. Photo: Kirk Hargreaves

This page: The Deans homestead, Homebush, near Darfield, lies in ruins the day after the quake. Photo: David Hallett **Following pages:** The quake caused plenty of damage to the St John's church in Hororata. Photo: Iain McGregor

Angus Donaldson Printers on Colombo Street, Sydenham, the morning of the quake. Photo: Carys Monteath

This page top: An electrical fire on Worcester Street. Photo: Iain McGregor **Bottom:** Sumner residents drove up Summit Road for fear of a tsunami. Photo: Iain McGregor **Opposite page:** Flooding in New Brighton. Photo: Iain McGregor

After the Quake

At 4.35am on Saturday, September 4, Canterbury and its people were changed forever. Martin van Beynen *looks back at the days after the earthquake, one of the region's most momentous weeks — and the miracle of survival that accompanied it.*

More than most disasters, an earthquake finds a city out.

A severe shake tests infrastructure, examines emergency responses, exposes planning decisions and, most of all, it asks some searching questions of its people.

Canterbury, in its first week after the major tremor, which struck at 4.35am on September 4, passed many of these tests with flying colours. It should give itself a collective pat on the back — but not too hard.

Within hours of the tremor, the airport had inspected its runways and aircraft were taking off again. The Port of Lyttelton was working again on Sunday afternoon despite up to $50 million damage to wharves and storage areas.

A week after one of the biggest jolts to strike a modern, populated city anywhere in the world, Canterbury authorities had managed to restore most of the services usually taken for granted.

A week after the quake, just about everybody still living in their own home in Canterbury had water and power. Given the extent of the original breakages and outages, that was some achievement. In fact, most homes had water and power by the first Monday night after the quake and by Tuesday, 90 per cent of the city's residents were able to flush their toilets.

As expected, Canterbury people pitched in and did what they could for themselves and their neighbours and friends. The welfare centres set up the first day and were still busy midweek with about 280 people in occupation, but closed down within the fortnight. Out of the city of 380,000 or so, that is not a large number.

People like bungy king A J Hackett went ahead with their weddings in the ruined city. Mike Bird didn't have much choice. He had already tattooed September 4 on his arm.

By Wednesday, the chooks had started laying again and by Thursday, several schools had re-opened. Not all the memories were bad. A few

> A severe shake tests infrastructure, examines emergency responses, exposes planning decisions and, most of all, it asks some searching questions of its people.

hours after the quake, writer Joe Bennett found his fellow citizens of Lyttelton in good spirits. "Everyone was talking in the sunshine. There was a lot of laughter. It didn't seem to be the nervous laughter of survivors. It was cheerful, convivial. It felt like a holiday," he wrote.

Opposite page: Xavier Trousselot-Rhodes (16) suffered cuts and bruises after falling one storey from his bedroom and being hit by flying bricks and debris as his home, the historic Hororata Homestead, about 30 km west of Christchurch, came near to collapse. Photo: Tony Benny

> **For many, the noise was deafening as windows rattled fit to break, glass and crockery crashed to the floor and chimneys and tiles toppled.**

In the aftermath, Wayne Alexander, of Christchurch, said: "You're never more in love with life and that's what I like about it. Whenever you face loss, you realise on the other side of it what you've got."

But first there was terror. For many, the noise was deafening as windows rattled fit to break, glass and crockery crashed to the floor and chimneys and tiles toppled. For many in the beach suburbs, the first panicked thought was of a possible tsunami. Those who had access to their vehicles caused a traffic jam as they headed away from the coast. Without power, many could not open their automatic garage doors.

Annette Preen, living on her own in her new house in Bexley, felt trapped as she tried to kick down her security door. "I thought I was going to die." When she made it outside, she fell headfirst into the wet sand piled at her front door.

"I fell flat on my face and the silt being so heavy, I couldn't get out."

For Chris Piper, 18, of St Martins, it was the scariest moment of his life. He was sleeping in a sleepout behind his family's home and was woken painfully when a television fell on his feet.

"I threw my girlfriend on the lawn and then went to the house in bare feet and my underwear to see tiles and the chimney crashing down. I thought the whole house was going to collapse. I thought my whole family was going to die in front of me."

Imagine the plight of paraplegic Renee Hayman, lying in her room at the Kate Sheppard Hospital in Avonside. "I felt quite helpless, really."

At dawn, Christchurch turned on a pearler of a day. Residents could survey the damage in the light of warm bright sunshine. Another godsend, perhaps.

Supermarkets were some of the first businesses to re-open. By 10.40am, St Martins New World had cleaned up aisles smelling of vinegar and alcohol and had tills running on generator power. By midday, power was on again and business was as lively as a Christmas Eve, owner Russell McKenzie said.

Other supermarkets around town dealt with panic buying and were soon out of bottled water, milk, bread, batteries and candles. As it became clear starvation was going to be averted, the panic subsided. Frantic buying at the city's service stations also abated as people realised fuel supplies were not threatened.

Every city has its low-lifes and a few took advantage of deserted houses and businesses to help themselves. Some were caught, including two burglars masquerading as tradesmen. Looting did not occur and overall crime was actually down, police said. However, domestic violence spiked as strained nerves and arguments escalated into punches and kicks.

COMMUNITY SPIRIT

The rally happened quickly. By midweek the army of volunteers, recruited partly from students at Canterbury's two universities and from the Christchurch Polytechnic, had swelled to more than 1000. Many others had already done their bit.

As Janet Derham prepared to evacuate her ravaged Bexley home on Monday, a woman from Avonhead and a student arrived from nowhere to help her pack. Age Concern had many offers from people offering to help old people clean up. Farmers near Darfield with working milking sheds helped neighbours whose sheds were not operating.

Mostly, the speedy restoration of services was due to the unstinting efforts of well-organised crews of fixers — the linesmen, the cable jointers, the excavator drivers, the drainlayers, the

---

Opposite page: The facade of Lyttelton's Empire Hotel in danger of falling. Photo: Kirk Hargreaves

Top: St Albans Seafood shop all but demolished. Photo: Iain McGregor **Bottom:** A local outside crumbling shops on Cranford Street. Photo: Iain McGregor

Top: Corner of Edgeware Road and Barbadoes Street, Edgeware. Photo: Iain McGregor. **Bottom:** An exposed room on Sherborne Street, St Albans.
Photo: Iain McGregor

plumbers, roofers and builders. They were people like Ed Askew, a cable jointer for Orion, the operator of the Christchurch power network, who worked continuous 14-hour days despite his own two-storey home being devastated. Orion engineer Steve MacDonald was at work at midday on Saturday despite the destruction of his home at Brooklands.

As a radio announcer put it: "Good people doing the right things."

> "We are not looking at a levelled city, but we are coming to terms with the damage, which is a bit like an iceberg — there may be structural damage underneath."
>
> — *Christchurch Mayor Bob Parker*

Christchurch City Council water and waste water manager Mark Christison said his workers repaired as many defects in six days as they would in a whole year.

A team of about 100 structural engineers from around the country assessed central city buildings for damage to allow people to return to offices and factories. On Thursday they turned their attention to houses. Police and army staff did the tedious work of staffing cordons and providing security. Volunteer firefighters tackled the thousands of teetering chimneys left in the wake of the earthquake.

AFTERSHOCK STRESS

As if there wasn't enough destruction and heartache caused by Saturday's jolt, on Wednesday Sentember 8, it all started again. At 7.49am, the region was rocked again by a shallow quake, at a depth of only 6 km, as sharp if not as long as the weekend's shake. It was the worst of more than 1000 aftershocks following the first tremor.

For some, it was one jolt too far. Cars streamed out of the city going both south and north. Mayor Bob Parker said that jolt had sent his "guts churning".

"It is like living in a maelstrom. This is a hammer blow to the spirit of a lot of people."

Hornby mother Nicola Sanderson sent her sleepless seven-year-old, Tony, to stay with his grandmother in Dunedin. Health communications specialist Kim Thomas took her 10-month-old baby to family in Napier. Beds at Christchurch Hospital were pushed together so patients could hold hands.

For some, the Lyttelton tremor was a tipping point. Steve Wragg, of Christchurch, was staying home. "You don't like to admit you are terrified," he said. Employers reported everyone being more jittery after the latest shake. Some workers refused to come to work.

The jolt of Wednesday, which centred in Lyttelton, worsened existing damage and caused more of its own. Power was cut temporarily and the Lyttelton Tunnel, which showed no damage after Saturday's quake, was closed for a couple of hours after cracks appeared in its tiles.

That afternoon, *Press* staff had to move out of their building in Cathedral Square for the first time. Buildings, already assessed twice since the Saturday shake, had to be reviewed again, and the state of emergency in Christchurch and Waimakariri was extended for seven days. It was eventually lifted on September 17, 13 days after the initial quake.

KEEPING UP APPEARANCES

Although the aftershocks kept coming, it was important to look around occasionally for a reminder that Christchurch was not levelled.

Opposite page: The Medway Street footbridge from River Road to Avonside Drive in Avonside. Photo: Dean Kozanic

Most of it looked absurdly normal. A stranger driving into Christchurch on Monday might well have wondered what all the fuss was about. A visitor would have seen the rubbish collectors emptying the city's red refuse bins, heavy traffic on intact roads and cyclists and joggers out enjoying a sunny day.

Structural damage such as that of the Canterbury earthquake is not instantly visible. The sharp-eyed would see tarpaulins covering holes where chimneys had stood, but would have been hard-pressed to see much more.

However, those inclined to scoff at media reports about the severity of the quake were in for a rude shock in the central city, where a different scene greeted the eye.

Police officers and army staff manned cordons and checkpoints. The streets crawled with men in white hard hats and orange vests carrying clipboards. Demolition crews were already working. Orange cones, temporary fences, emergency tape and orange netting screened hard-hit buildings, many sporting jagged cracks and missing facades. A walk around town, to those parts that were accessible, would have revealed cracked towers, ruptured walls and piles of rubble.

LUCKY ESCAPE

The Canterbury earthquake will be remembered for the massive damage it caused rather than the people it killed. The absence of loss of life is its distinguishing characteristic. In the Haiti earthquake in January, which clocked much the same mark on the Richter scale, 250,000 were killed. The Kobe earthquake (7.1) in Japan in 1995 claimed 6400 lives. The Napier earthquake in February 1931 killed 256 people and even the Murchison quake of 1929 had 17 fatalities. But in Canterbury the death toll was 0.

Some of the zero total can be put down to pure luck. Mayor Bob Parker described it as "the most extraordinary miraculous event".

The timing of the first 30-second jolt on Saturday was incredibly fortunate. The Napier earthquake hit at about 10.30am on a busy shopping day.

> "When I got to work at five this morning I couldn't hear the birds chirping. That's how I knew the earthquakes were still around."
>
> — *Hotel worker Hessie Toms*

In Christchurch the streets were empty of traffic and people. Nobody was shopping and few cars were parked under the many brick facades in the city. Nobody, for instance, was on the footpath outside the apartments of the former Old Normal School building in Montreal Street when a massive chimney came tumbling onto the asphalt.

Nobody was sleeping in the guest bedroom at the historic Godley House, in Diamond Harbour, when the fireplace fell onto the bed. Nobody was on Bridle Path Road near Lyttelton when a car-sized boulder plummeted from its perch further up the hill. Renowned architect Sir Miles Warren was not sitting in his usual chair at his historic homestead Ohinetahi when stone blocks landed on it.

More importantly, nobody was working in the Hornby coolstores and supermarket distribution centres where nine-metre-high racking loaded with heavy goods collapsed. The resulting mess in some warehouses was three storeys high, but at least nobody was buried underneath.

Debris from the warehouses was soon clogging the city's transfer stations. One operation lost tens of millions of dollars' worth

Opposite page top: Army help police on central city cordons. Looking south down Colombo Street from Armagh Street. Photo: Iain McGregor
Bottom: A building inspector puts a yellow ticket (restricted use) on the Octagon restaurant on the corner of Manchester and Worcester streets. Photo: Iain McGregor

Demolition workers clear the site of a badly damaged building on the corner of Manchester and Worcester streets.

Buildings with no access

Buildings with restricted access

Kilmore St

Chester St West

Colombo St

Madras St

Chester St East

Durham St North

Armagh St

Manchester St

Gloucester St

Oxford Tce

Cathedral Square

Worcester St

Latimer Square

Colombo St

Hereford St

Madras St

Cashel St

High St

Bedford Row

Lichfield St

of alcohol. Another large New Zealand-wide coolstore business lost $40 million worth of frozen goods including most of the country's stock of frozen turkeys.

DEVASTATION MINIMISED

Former Christchurch man John Mander, a structural engineering professor teaching at Texas A&M University, says "of any place in the world this would probably be the best prepared".

He refers to the more stringent building standards imposed in New Zealand after the Napier earthquake and to the general awareness gained from living in an earthquake-prone country.

There is no doubt Canterbury responded extremely well. A well-educated and resourceful population containing an army of skill and brawn, backed by a trained and honest central and local government, civil service, police force and other emergency services made all the difference. Canterbury is not Haiti, which showed the world that poverty kills.

Modern technology also helped. Earthquake-proof cellphone towers meant people could check on each other and call for help.

Valerie Walsh, for instance, was stuck in the dark in her twisted Bexley house, which was slowly filling with silty water. She texted a friend who sounded the alert.

Websites, including *The Press*'s online service, were able to provide vital information about water and sewerage, especially when power was re-established. Radio stations did a marvellous job of keeping people informed.

The fact the quake's devastation was localised to parts of the city meant that friends and family were able to help those less fortunate. The lack of serious injuries and people trapped in buildings eased what could have been an enormous load on the emergency services.

EMERGENCY SERVICES

Hospitals and medical centres were able to cope as they dealt with about 100 cases of earthquake-related injuries. Had it been worse, the emergency services could have called on some 525 of the nation's general practitioners who were in Christchurch for their annual conference.

In addition, only small fires broke out.

In Napier, even sound buildings were destroyed by a huge blaze that spread quickly in the wind and heat because firefighters were unable to use their hoses due to a water-pressure collapse. Christchurch firefighters had to put out only one fire, a blaze in JoJo's massage parlour, which broke out when Prime Minister John Key was inspecting the damage in Worcester Street with Mayor Bob Parker.

The Big One was supposed to come from the Alpine Fault, which is due for a pressure release.

SEISMIC SUSCEPTIBILITY

Strangely, Christchurch is not particularly earthquake prone. Look at a New Zealand map denoting the big shakes between 1870 and 1980 with red dots and Christchurch is blank. The Big One was supposed to come from the Alpine Fault, which is due for a pressure release. Instead, the quake of September 4 came from a fault hidden under the Canterbury gravels near Darfield, about 40 km west of Christchurch. The fault had not moved much for 16,000 years. When it shed its load, its tentacles reached out in arbitrary directions, sparing some areas but ruining others.

The area closest to the epicentre, fortunately most of it rural and largely unpopulated, showed how violently the earth had moved. A double row of young trees in the middle of the 30 km fault trace, from Greendale to Aylesbury, moved 4.5 metres. As the quake fanned out it buckled railway tracks near Sandy Knolls Road corner and shifted the centre lines of Telegraph Road to the side of the road. The area experienced the strongest ground shaking ever recorded in New Zealand.

On farms, tracks, water races, fences and shelter belts were displaced. About 45 grain silos tipped over and rotary dairy sheds jumped their rails. At a poultry farm in Weedons 3000 egg-laying chooks were killed when two or three stands containing their 26,000 chickens collapsed. In Greendale 300 tonnes of sorted potatoes in a storage shed were turned into a jumbled mess on the shed floor.

> "Many have worked 14-hour days, every day since the quake. Some have had their own homes destroyed but have stayed at work."
>
> *— Roger Sutton, Orion chief executive*

One fork of the fault headed on a line towards Christchurch city and its suburbs, branching up to strike Kaiapoi, 20 km north of Christchurch, which displayed some of the most graphic damage after the quake.

The city suburbs of Avonside, Bexley, Burwood, New Brighton, Dallington, all built predominantly on ocean and river sand were ravaged by liquefaction, a phenomenon that turns the ground's underlying layers to jelly.

With a force only nature can produce, silt/sand-laden water was forced through the ground under houses. Steel reinforced concrete pads under new houses cracked and shifted under the strain. Older houses on piles moved off their foundations. Roads in the worst affected areas buckled and crumpled and some powerpoles dropped several metres. Small but productive sand volcanoes appeared all over the area spreading a thick layer of wet sand and silt onto gardens, streets and footpaths. The Avon River bed rose

as if an underground snake had burrowed its way along its course. Pipes of every description broke and water mixed with sewage in the streets. A bridge in Kaiapoi collapsed and a walking bridge in Avonside twisted to resemble a corkscrew.

INFRASTRUCTURE

A city is only as good as its infrastructure. Christchurch's proved remarkably resilient, thanks partly to a lot of precautionary work.

As dawn broke on Saturday all of rural Canterbury was out of power as was 90 per cent of the city. By Tuesday only 1000 properties still lacked power, but by the end of the week almost everyone was reconnected.

Orion chief executive Roger Sutton, who had worked over 100 hours in the week after the quake, said the company's 500 staff had been nothing short of phenomenal.

"Many have worked 14-hour days, every day since the quake. Some have had their own homes destroyed but have stayed at work.

"Everyone pitched in. What's kept them going is helping their fellow Cantabrians. Getting the power back as soon as humanly possible. Knowing that lights and heating and the TV and all those things make a big, big difference to how people feel. It's also been heart-wrenching at times too, having to cut off the power to homes and businesses that are being demo-lished. Our call centre staff have [dealt with] people in tears."

Despite new artesian wells opening up all over the city, the quake also deprived large parts of Christchurch of drinking water. About 60 streets were still without water on Wednesday, September 8, but by Thursday night, after rigorous testing assisted by the army, the warning to boil all water was lifted everywhere except in isolated areas of the Waimakariri District.

The Bromley waste-water treatment plant worked and the Christchurch ocean outfall was

---

Opposite page: Kerry McCarthy sits with daughter Maeve (4) and watches the Valley Inn pub get knocked down. Photo: Iain McGregor

out of action briefly because of the power outage but quickly came back into operation.

OUT OF HOUSE AND HOME

One of the main casualties of the quake is housing. By Tuesday September 7, the Earthquake Commission had totted up 22,000 claims for damage to homes. By the end of the week that total had gone past 40,000 and was growing. The EQC expects close to 100,000 claims to arise from the earthquake.

In the short term those with unsafe homes bunked in with family and friends, and others used welfare centres, but long-term solutions are needed. The quake showed that some areas of Christchurch should never have been used for housing in the first place. For instance, it exposed the 150-section Pacific Park in Bexley as a disaster waiting to happen.

The human cost was enormous. Some, like Sue and Don Rutter, had just moved into dream homes. The Dalleys, a retired couple in Bexley, had just planted their potatoes.

"We loved living here. Every day was precious. In the meantime we will become gypsies. I don't know what will happen. Who needs this at our age?" Janet Dalley said.

BUSINESS

Once the dust settled over the region and in the central city, it was clear business and livelihoods would be profoundly affected. Estimates of the damage went quickly from $2 billion to $4b and upwards. Prime Minister John Key says the Government will pick up 85–90 per cent of the tab.

The central city was off limits to 50,000 workers on Monday, September 6, and, although the cordon shrank, much of the core of the city was still unreachable at the end of the week. Many businesses that eventually re-opened would face weeks of lost revenue.

During closure, workers still had to be paid.

On the Tuesday after the quake, the Government helped with a $15m package for emergency wages, providing a wage subsidy of $350 gross per week for workers in businesses unable to open. It also ploughed $5m into the Mayoral Relief Fund and was putting about $90m into roading.

Banks alleviated some concerns by providing softer loans and overdraft facilities and the council declared a short rates holiday. Some businesses closed for good and some, like the New World at Kaiapoi, which made its 90 staff redundant, and the town's historic department store Blackwells, will take a year to rebuild.

As a result of drawing a wider net, shares in New Zealand insurance companies were marked down and the Christchurch City Council and its holding company CCHL had their AA+ issuer credit rating placed on watch.

Despite the rush on some supplies after the quake, shopping dropped off the list of priorities. Eftpos sales were slashed by a third over the weekend.

Yet for most of Canterbury's large companies, like Tait Industries which employs about 800 people, it was business as usual.

Canterbury Employers Chamber of Commerce chief executive Peter Townsend said it was important to remember 80 per cent of Christchurch was getting on with the job.

HERITAGE LOST

Heritage buildings throughout the region suffered a terrible blow. Christchurch was home to probably Australasia's best example of Gothic architecture and an application to have the city declared a World Heritage site was in train. The city is notable for its range of architectural styles including the Chicago School style Manchester Courts, built in 1905 in Manchester Street, which will be demolished as a result of the quake.

On Monday, September 6, engineers inspected 678 buildings in the central city, of

which about 40 received a red 'no go' sticker.

On the positive side, due to strengthening, several major historic buildings held up well.

Christ Church Cathedral and the Catholic Basilica, both recently strengthened, survived intact, as did the Canterbury Museum and the Provincial Chambers. The Arts Centre sustained some expensive and serious damage but nothing that cannot be repaired.

Not all were so lucky. Lyttelton's Holy Trinity Anglican Church, the oldest stone church in Canterbury, and the Durham Street Methodist Church, the oldest stone church in Christchurch, were in a parlous state with major structural cracking. The Repertory Theatre in Kilmore Street lost its facade and buildings such as the Memorial Hall (1929) at Lincoln University, have been lost.

The amount of red brick rubble on the streets on Saturday signalled the blow to Christchurch's red brick architecture, much of it built between 1880 and the Depression and, of course, "non-engineered". The high brick tower of the former Christchurch Railway station in Moorhouse Avenue was badly cracked under its clock.

"Brick is the warm infill between our grey heritage buildings and hard geometry of the modern. Without our red brick our urban environment will become increasingly sterile," architect Peter Beaven said.

By the end of the week brick shops and restaurants were coming down. People wept as their businesses crumbled under the sweep of the excavator's arm.

Some of the region's finest old homesteads, remnants of the region's founders and landed aristocracy — Glenroy, Homebush, Hororata, Purau Homestead, Godley House — sustained potentially fatal damage.

Modern buildings in the city were not immune either. The Copthorne Hotel was closed to guests due to concerns about core damage and the 17-storey Clarendon Towers in

Worcester Street was closed. The city council's new building in Hereford Street also had damage to its internal stairs and had to be closed for several days.

LOOKING FORWARD

The citizens of Canterbury realise that the focus must now be on the future. The first priority will be replacing the lost housing and ensuring livelihoods are re-established. The region will get a brisk economic stimulus from the clean-up and rebuilding. Some have already pointed to the benefit of the region getting a new infrastructure courtesy of the insurance industry.

> ## "Without our red brick our urban environment will become increasingly sterile."
>
> *— Christchurch architect Peter Beaven*

The quake also means Canterbury is much better prepared and equipped for its next big earthquake. Opposition to tighter building regulations and earthquake strengthening will now be an isolated whisper in the region.

Clearly, some of the city's risky buildings have been exposed and expunged without loss of life and the city has received a brusque reminder about where it is safe to build. The quake and its aftermath will be studied and analysed for years to come. For New Zealand it is a resounding wake-up call.

And for Cantabrians, whether they suffered damage or not, the earthquake of September 4 was a shattering experience never to be forgotten.

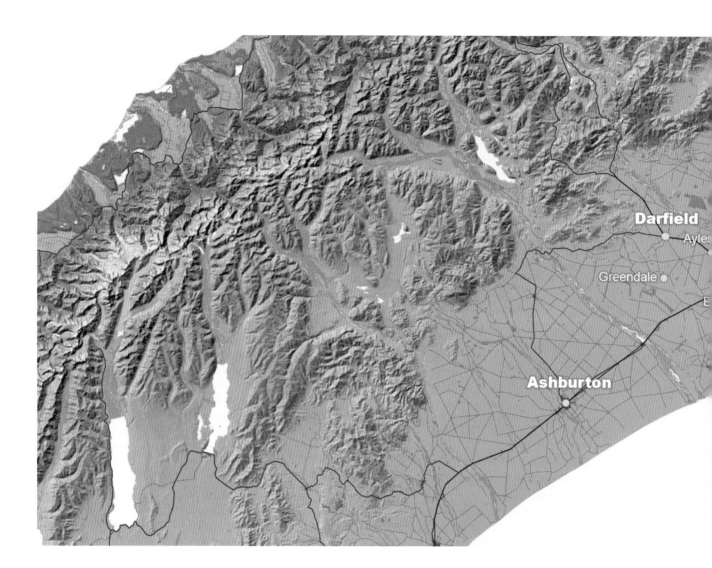

Darfield
Ayles
Greendale
Ashburton

The Science of the Quake

The Canterbury earthquake took many by surprise but some scientists have been warning for years about the risk of hidden faults under the Canterbury Plains. Paul Gorman *looks at the science behind the quake and its effects on the landscape.*

The September 4 earthquake was the result of not one but three earthquakes, just seconds apart, ripping a 25-kilometre gash across the Canterbury Plains and unleashing energy equivalent to the detonation of 670,000 tonnes of explosives.

In the wake of the 7.1 magnitude earthquake, GNS Science geologists have discovered a new fault trace running roughly west–east between

Greendale and a point halfway between Aylesbury and Burnham.

Aerial surveys measured the new trace as 22 km long, but ground mapping has extended it further and revealed an extra strand extending to close to Rolleston.

Some scientists believe it has been at least 16,000 years since the "blind-thrust fault", hidden under the gravels of the Canterbury Plains, deposited that many years ago at the end of the last glaciation, last ruptured. The fault had been accumulating stress for thousands of years and scientists are now keen to learn if the underground fault extends beyond the visible surface rupture.

The earthquake will have released most of the energy from that fault and is also likely to have taken some of the strain energy off other main

Kaiapoi

Christchurch CBD

Lyttelton

Akaroa

"Before Saturday, there was nothing in the landscape that would have suggested there was an active fault beneath the Darfield and Rolleston areas"

— *Dr Kelvin Berryman, GNS Science*

faults in the region. The tremor shattered roads, broke water races and shunted shelterbelts and fences about three metres to the right. It has also lifted land up to a metre in places.

More than 1000 aftershocks rattled Canterbury in the weeks following September 4, some more than five in magnitude. Cantabrians became very familiar with the stomach-tightening rumble that announces the arrival of a new shock.

Scientists are also investigating what has been called a foreshock of about magnitude 5.4 just a few seconds before the main quake. Canterbury University geological sciences lecturer Dr Mark Quigley believes it is possible the dormant Hororata Fault may also have moved but it is unclear whether it caused the 7.1 event or whether it was in response to it.

There were three distinct pulses of energy around 4.35am on Saturday, September 4, but seismic energy from the two shocks became entangled, making it difficult initially to pinpoint the size, location and depth of the main shock.

The foreshock awoke some sleeping

The surface of the Earth is divided into seven major plates and several minor ones. They move a few centimetres a year riding on semi-molten layers of rock underneath the crust. As the plates move they pull apart or collide, setting the scene for volcanoes, earthquakes and other geological activity.

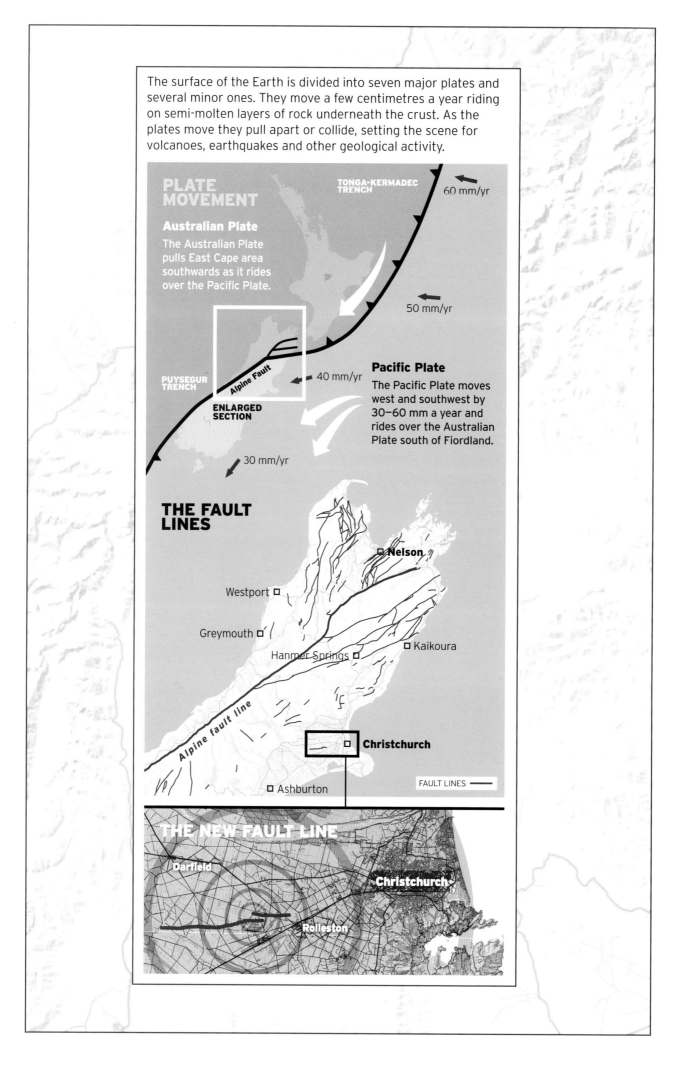

PLATE MOVEMENT

Australian Plate
The Australian Plate pulls East Cape area southwards as it rides over the Pacific Plate.

TONGA-KERMADEC TRENCH

60 mm/yr

50 mm/yr

PUYSEGUR TRENCH

Alpine Fault

40 mm/yr

ENLARGED SECTION

Pacific Plate
The Pacific Plate moves west and southwest by 30–60 mm a year and rides over the Australian Plate south of Fiordland.

30 mm/yr

THE FAULT LINES

Nelson

Westport

Greymouth

Hanmer Springs

Kaikoura

Alpine fault line

Christchurch

FAULT LINES ▬▬▬

Ashburton

THE NEW FAULT LINE

Darfield

Christchurch

Rolleston

Cantabrians and gave them a few seconds' advance notice of the main shake. The location of the first shake is still being debated.

Even though earthquake geologists had

Alarming aftershocks on the night of September 6–7 were followed by a violent and shallow 5.1 quake at 7.44am on September 8

warned about Canterbury's hidden faults, the sudden appearance of the Greendale Fault was a major surprise that could require a revision of the region's building design standards.

Alarming aftershocks on the night of September 6–7 were followed by a violent and shallow 5.1 quake at 7.44am on September 8

that gave residents living in southern parts of Christchurch and around Lyttelton Harbour a real fright. The shake was centred on another fault somewhere near the city exit of the Lyttelton road tunnel and had scientists scratching their heads. It has also been followed by smaller aftershocks centred near or underneath the city. Nearby, increased outflow from warm springs at the northern end of Rapaki Bay and wafting sulphurous smells had some worrying that the Lyttelton volcano which last erupted 5.8 million years ago might be coming back to life. However, scientists said there was no evidence of any magma activity underneath the harbour.

One of the most visible effects of the earthquake in Christchurch was soil liquefaction, which caused much of the damage to homes and roads in eastern suburbs. Engineers have warned about the dangers of liquefaction in a major earthquake for many years but this is the first time it has occurred on such a wide scale.

Above: An aerial view of the quake epicentre. Farmers at the epicentre were quick to comment (and counter-comment) on the fact that the quake occurred at a previously unknown fault line.

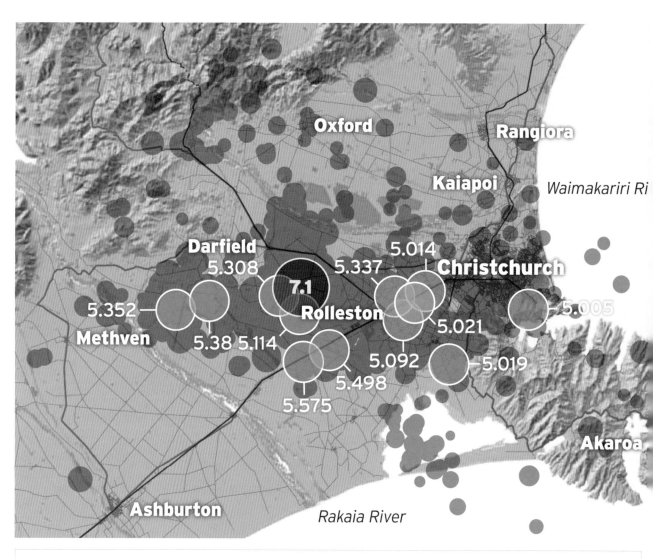

Oxford

Rangiora

Kaiapoi

Waimakariri Ri

Darfield
5.308

5.014

5.337

Christchurch

7.1

5.352

Rolleston

5.005

Methven

5.38 5.114

5.021

5.092

5.019

5.498

5.575

Akaroa

Ashburton

Rakaia River

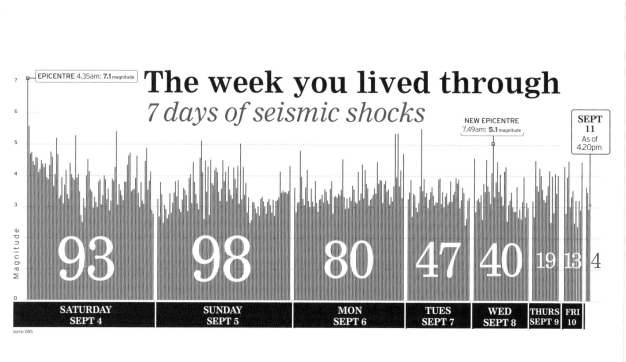

EPICENTRE 4.35am: **7.1** magnitude

The week you lived through
7 days of seismic shocks

NEW EPICENTRE
7.49am: **5.1** magnitude

SEPT
11
As of
4.20pm

Magnitude

93 | 98 | 80 | 47 | 40 | 19 | 13 | 4

| SATURDAY SEPT 4 | SUNDAY SEPT 5 | MON SEPT 6 | TUES SEPT 7 | WED SEPT 8 | THURS SEPT 9 | FRI 10 |

Source: GNS

Quake locations and magnitudes

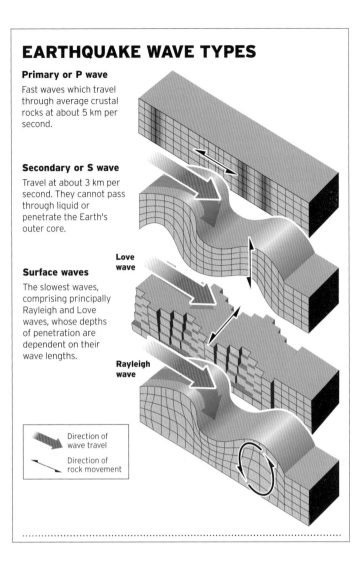

EARTHQUAKE WAVE TYPES

Primary or P wave
Fast waves which travel through average crustal rocks at about 5 km per second.

Secondary or S wave
Travel at about 3 km per second. They cannot pass through liquid or penetrate the Earth's outer core.

Surface waves
The slowest waves, comprising principally Rayleigh and Love waves, whose depths of penetration are dependent on their wave lengths.

Love wave

Rayleigh wave

Direction of wave travel

Direction of rock movement

Properties in the not so hard-hit western half of the city sit mainly on stony, gravelly soils, while those further east are on loosely compacted, sandy soils. The earthquake caused liquefaction of sand and small "sand volcanoes" in many suburbs. The material under houses, roads and other structures made a big difference to how they reacted to major shaking. In the eastern suburbs the soil predominantly has a sand base — river sand in some places and beach sand in others. At various depths within the top four to five metres of ground there are layers of sand which were deposited naturally and are quite loose, with the space between the soil occupied by water. The shaking of a significant earthquake pushes the sand grains together and effectively squeezes the water to the surface, taking much of the sand with it.

In most areas this simply caused a mess, but in areas along rivers, the liquefied layer provided a weak layer on top of which more rigid soil slid down into the river. This was particularly evident along the Avon.

Most of the other damage was the result of shaking, accompanied by possible minor liquefaction, to old-style masonry buildings predominantly in the city centre.

According to GNS Science, the September 4 quake on the Canterbury Plains was a low-probability event.

Seismologists believe the major earthquake risk to Christchurch still comes from known faults in North Canterbury, in the Canterbury foothills, and from the Alpine Fault up the spine of the South Island.

Top: Many of the residents of Seabreeze Close and neighbouring streets in Bexley had to pack up due to the severity of damage. Shelly Sutherland, left, helps Kerry Donald clear his belongings from his house. Photo: Dean Kozanic **Bottom:** Water forced to the surface by the earthquake produced thousands of small volcano-like structures on the Avon River estuary. Similar structures burst through the ground throughout eastern suburbs. Photo: John McCombe

Top: Waitaki Street resident Mark Gilbertson shovels silt. The crater on this New Brighton street was made when the footpath collapsed, breaking water mains and flooding the street. Photo: Charlie Gates **Bottom left:** The Kobussen family all pitched in to clear their grandmother's Kaiapoi driveway. From left to right: Josh (11), Henny and Luke (14). Photo: Carys Monteath **Right:** Jo Mackwell digs silt out of her parents' garden in Reaby Street, Burwood. Photo: Dean Kozanic

Top: A car in Hoon Hay Road was crushed by a falling chimney during the quake. Photo: Jono Smit **Bottom:** Paul Ward looks at damage in his Avonside Drive home from which he has had to move. Photo: Iain McGregor

Top: Chris Lamb surveys the damage across his lawn in Christchurch after the September 4 earthquake. Photo: Charlie Gates **Bottom:** Simon Jones moving out of his Brooklands home. Photo: Iain McGregor

Top: Major damage to St Paul's Church on Gayhurst Road, Dallington. The building was condemned. Photo: Iain McGregor **Bottom:** A court at the Tai Tapu Tennis Club, Tai Tapu Domain. Photo: Canterbury Tennis

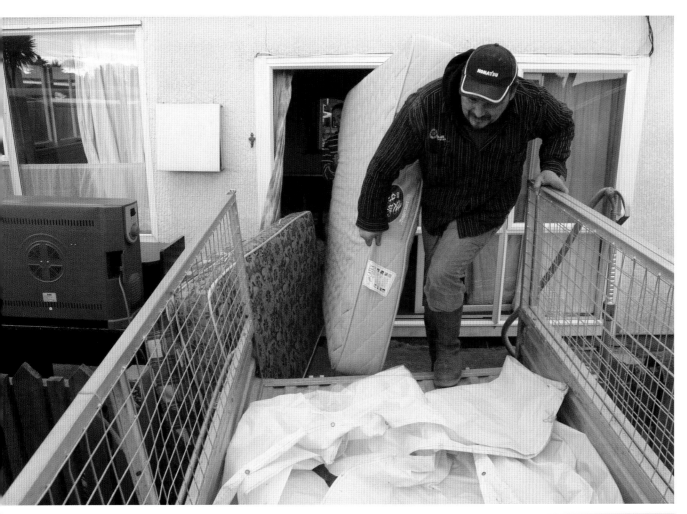

Top: The day after the earthquake, Shane Hicks moves to a motel in the fear that his Pine Beach house is condemned. Photo: Kirk Hargreaves
Bottom: Christine Collins moving out of her home on Avonside Drive, September 4. Photo: Iain McGregor

Top: Damage to the recently restored Lyttelton Timeball Station. Photo: Martin van Beynen **Bottom:** William Cottrell in his bedroom in Gunyah homestead, Glenroy, from which he escaped the earthquake. Photo: David Hallett

Top: New Brighton petrol station owner Sam Parks surveys earthquake damage. Photo: Martin Hunter **Bottom:** A hedge split by the fault line showing horizontal displacement. Photo: Richard Cosgrove

A house on stilts collapsed near Hororata. Photo: Iain McGregor

Top: Firefighters were busy in Kaiapoi the day after the 7.1 quake, pulling down suspect chimneys with northwest winds predicted to reach galeforce.
Photo: Kirk Hargreaves **Bottom:** Gayhurst Road running off Avonside Drive. The road was torn apart by the quake. Photo: Luke Thomas

Top: Fissures in the road at the Belfast/Marshlands Main North Road motorway on-ramp. Photo: Carys Monteath **Bottom:** A damaged swing bridge over Kaiapoi River. Photo: Martin Hunter

Earthquake damage to roads near Darfield. Photo: Martin Hunter

This page top: Wunderbar co-owner Andrew Bishop hopes to have the iconic Lyttelton bar running again by New Year's Eve. Photo: Elliot Sim **Centre:** The Valley Inn in Heathcote is demolished. Shane Spence from Beardsley Contractor salvages the Tui sign. Photo: Iain McGregor **Bottom:** Lion Nathan staff clean up a warehouse in St Asaph Street. Even though there was huge destruction, beer supplies were restored with the arrival of 55 shipping containers filled with beer from Auckland. Photo: Richard Cosgrove

Opposite page top: An exposed wall in shops on Colombo Street between Kilmore Street and Peterborough Street. Photo: Iain McGregor **Bottom:** Demolition on Victoria Street. Photo: David Hallett

The Jacobsen Tiles building (formerly Maddison's Pub) on the corner of Moorhouse Avenue and Montreal Street has its top roof section pulled off after it became unsafe in Wednesday's aftershock. Photo: Richard Cosgrove

Top: The cast iron decoration being removed from The Press building turret after it was declared unsafe. Photo: Stacy Squires **Bottom:** Blackwell's department store, a Kaiapoi landmark, was deemed too dangerous and the careful demolition took place on September 4. Photo: Carys Monteath

Top: The corner of Victoria Street and Bealey Avenue where Knox Church still stands. Across the road the Daily Bagel and Covent Fruit Store shops are demolished. Photo: David Hallett **Bottom:** Demolition on Victoria Street near the corner of Bealey Avenue. Photo: Iain McGregor

Top: A building reduced to rubble on Manchester Street in the central city. Photo: David Hallett **Bottom:** The clean-up on Riccarton Road, September 10, 2010. Photo: David Hallett

This page top: Mike Kerr, owner of Vaughan Antiques shop, which was demolished. Photo: Iain McGregor Centre left: The front window of Enjoy restaurant, Victoria Street, showing the red sticker, which means it is condemned. Photo: Iain McGregor Right: Api Agsornwong, left, and Prakob Sresthakupt, right, the owners of condemned Enjoy Thai Restaurant on Victoria Street watch nearby buildings being demolished. Photo: Iain McGregor Bottom: Rose Lennon, owner of La Boutique, watches the demolition of buildings on the corner of Cranford and Westminster streets. Photo: Iain McGregor

Opposite page top: Aerial pictures of earthquake damage on Riccarton Road. Photo: David Hallett Bottom: Earthquake damage on Riccarton Road. Photo: David Hallett

Top: Teams of building inspectors gathered at the Linwood Service Centre before heading into the eastern suburbs. Jeanette Banks, centre right, shares the relief of having had her property inspected, with sister and Red Cross member Sandie Horne, down from Nelson. Napier building inspector, Gary Marshall, left, and City Council planner, Kent Wilson at right. Photo: Dean Kozanic Bottom: Members of the Red Cross civil defence response team and South Canterbury Police in Christchurch helping with the clean-up by a damaged bridge on River Road, Tai Tapu. Welfare checks required the team to walk along River Road checking on householders. Photo: John Bisset

Top: Whole blocks of buildings on Riccarton Road from Straven Road west were sealed off. USAR members Dr Jan Kupec, left, and Mike Stewart, on Riccarton Road. Photo: Dean Kozanic **Bottom left:** Halswell School principal Bruce Topham, right, and engineer Malcolm Freeman, look at damage done to the school. Photo: David Hallett **Right:** Mana Tamaiparea fills water bottles at a civil defence centre at Kaiapoi North School. Photo: Kirk Hargreaves

Owen Trowbridge (16) walks through a deep crack in Kaiapoi. Photo: Iain McGregor

Top: Duncan Noble, Master's student, left, and Tim Stahl, PhD student, measuring an earthquake-induced fracture in the Harper Hills northwest of Hororata. Photo: John Kirk-Anderson **Bottom:** Tim Stahl maps the fault line west of Rolleston with GPS equipment. Photo: David Hallett

Top: Volunteers, Siena Childs (13) left, Sam Butcher (13), Jess Butcher (18) and Alex Summerlee (18) clean up in Avonside Drive following the Canterbury earthquake. Photo: John Kirk-Anderson **Bottom:** Home-made signs mark earthquake damage in Spencerville. Photo: Martin Hunter

University Student Sam Johnson used Facebook to organise students to go into the suburbs to help residents clean up after the quake. Here they work in Halswell to help residents clear silt from their properties. Photo: Carys Monteath

Sam Bowen (9) and Emmaleigh Bowen (4) explore cracks in Raven Quay, Kaiapoi. Photo: Blair Ensor

Playing in cracks on Avonside Drive. From left: Bailey McFarlane (6), Cameron McFarlane (4) and Tyler McFarlane (9). Photo: Iain McGregor

Top: Navaeh Richard (3) with her mum Suzie Richard and sister Keisha (17 months) take refuge at Twiggers Restaurant at Addington Raceway. Photo: Kirk Hargreaves **Bottom:** Charlie Taraw, Tamatea Briggs (12) and Ngarita Briggs (8) sit under a makeshift shelter while they wait for a wood fire to boil water. They were too scared to go back into their Maling Street house in Avonside and instead slept on the lawn. Photo: Iain McGregor

Top: Eighty-nine-year-old Jean Sparks of Sockburn being lifted up stairs by firemen into Twiggers Restaurant at Addington Raceway. Photo: Kirk Hargreaves
Bottom: Too scared to go back to their house, the McLeod family take refuge at Linwood College. From left: Aaron McLeod, Lorraine McLeod and Grant McLeod. Photo: Iain McGregor

All Black captain Richie McCaw meets pupils of the badly damaged St Paul's School. Photo: Iain McGregor

This page top: City Care workers, from left, Donny Haenga, Mafutga and David Henry enjoy a barbecue put on by City Care for their staff. The trio, from Wellington, worked for over 100 hours between them in the three days after they arrived. Thirty-five specialists from Tauranga, Wellington, Dunedin and Timaru joined the Christchurch staff with trucks and equipment from around the country. Photo: Don Scott
Bottom: Maria Romero gave birth to Lola Mae during the September 4 earthquake. Romero was in a birthing pool in Christchurch Women's Hospital on the fifth floor when the quake struck. Photo: Carys Monteath

Opposite page top: Christ Church Cathedral holds its Sunday service in the Square.
Bottom: AJ Hackett and Amanda Hackett with a chandelier recovered by a Southern Demolition plant operator from her damaged shop, Shrimpton Radcliffe Design, on Victoria Street, following the quakes. Photo: John Kirk-Anderson

The Day the Quake Hit *The Press*

The Press journalists were jolted into action on Saturday, September 4, to report on an earthquake on their own doorstep. Deputy editor Coen Lammers looks back at how the newspaper reacted to the biggest local news story in its history.

The Canterbury earthquake of September 4 was not only a historic day for the region but also for *The Press* newspaper. The speed in which the newsroom staff reacted and started filing, despite their personal trauma, speaks volumes of their professionalism and commitment to their trade.

Just as the devastating 7.1 earthquake struck at 4.35am, most households were receiving their normal Saturday copy of *The Press*. After quickly assessing the safety of their family and property, journalists around the city jumped into gear. At 4.37am editor Andrew Holden informs Fairfax online staff that the city has been struck, before checking up on the health of his key staff.

With power cut throughout the city, online editor Colin Espiner fires up his laptop in total darkness in his Beckenham kitchen to break the news to the world. "The Telecom wireless network was a bit shaky, but with my aircard I managed to get our first story up on press.co.nz by 4.50am," said Espiner.

At that stage he already has received a call from science reporter Paul Gorman who has spoken to government science agency GNS, which informs him that Canterbury is dealing with a quake between 7.2 and 7.4 on the Richter scale. "I was taking notes on a piece of scrap paper by candlelight. I couldn't believe what I was hearing," recalled Gorman, still clinging on to his fragment of historical notes.

Online video editor Dan Tobin, who lives close to the CBD, is the first in the building, a mere 20 minutes after the quake. Even before the historic heritage building in Cathedral Square has been cleared by engineers, Tobin logs on and starts uploading his first pictures.

Staff from all sectors of *The Press* and its community papers found a temporary home at *The Press* printing plant on Logistics Drive after the main building had to be evacuated on September 8.

Operations manager Len McKenzie is next on site and quickly assesses that there is no structural damage.

The company's diesel generator has already kicked in and Tobin informs the rest of the news team that the building is safe. It is an island of light in a city cloaked in darkness.

He goes into town to start filming and his first impressions become most popular video on YouTube around the world for days after the quake.

Across town on the Huntsbury hill, chief reporter Kamala Hayman has received a text from editor Andrew Holden to see if she is okay "but I reckon he was just checking whether I was heading into work," Hayman laughed.

> "I was taking notes on a piece of scrap paper by candlelight. I couldn't believe what I was hearing."
>
> *Paul Gorman, science reporter for The Press*

During the quake, photographer Iain McGregor is thrown off his bed in the seaside suburb of Sumner. Once the shaking stops, he grabs his camera gear and heads for the hills fearing the quake was offshore and could cause a tsunami. He takes some shots of hundreds of scared residents heading for higher ground, but

races into work as soon as the radio confirms that the epicentre is about 40 km inland.

By then several reporters have already hit their local streets looking for updates. Rebecca Todd in New Brighton, Beck Eleven in Edgeware and Keith Lynch in St Albans. Lynch, a recent recruit from Ireland, does not realise what he is dealing with at first. "I had no idea, I thought someone was trying to get into my house. So I rang Paul (Gorman) who told me I had just been through an earthquake."

First Lynch rings his parents back home to tell them he has survived a major earthquake before contacting the police and filing a web update on looters getting caught in the inner city. He then drives around the neighbourhood to find major damage that could make good video or pictures before going into the office.

At work Lynch hooks up with photographer McGregor and tries to reach Avonside Drive, which has been particularly hard hit.

Like the other reporters, Martin van Beynen, who is checking out sites around his Banks Peninsula home, continuously files updates by phone and text message to Espiner, whose kitchen table has become the global epicentre of the internet.

Due to the power outage much of Christchurch is unable to find out what is happening, but most get updates from friends around the world who are glued to their televisions and computers, watching the story unfold on *The Press* website.

Once daylight arrives around 6am, Espiner

Left: Reporter Glenn Conway interviews Invercargill mayor Tim Shadbolt and Christchurch mayor Bob Parker. **Right:** The editorial team has an improvised news conference around some rubbish bins in their temporary home on Gloucester Street which normally houses the newspapers sales team.

decides to head into the office. He discovers his house has not been spared as his car backs over the remnants of the chimney in the driveway.

At the front door of *The Press* he bumps into freelance photographer Lance Burke who had partied through the night, but stumbled out of an inner-city pub once the shaking stopped, and started shooting. He offers some of the first, most compelling shots of the tragedy to *The Press*, which are quickly uploaded.

"Once I got into the seat, I did not move for another 12 hours," recalls Espiner.

As she arrives, Hayman is already surrounded by a host of reporters in the office and in the field.

Reporter Charlie Gates, who also fled from his seaside home to avoid a potential tsunami, joins Hayman to check out early casualties at the Christchurch Hospital and After Hours surgery.

Country reporter Marc Greenhill is on deck early to check the hotspots around the Canterbury hinterland which are particularly hard hit.

Back in town council reporter Sam Sachdeva also reports for duty and files the first updates around the infrastructure, the power and water issues that will dominate the early web news.

He then travels to Kaiapoi with photographer Carys Monteath, who had been one of the first on the road, recording the damage in her southern suburbs. In Kaiapoi, *The Press* team witness the destruction of the North Canterbury town, where

roads are flooded or covered in silt, and iconic buildings and bridges are trashed.

Picture editor Nigel Malthus, meanwhile, is flat out uploading and captioning the pictures that are brought in or emailed by photographers, reporters and the public. Malthus realises the illustrations editor is out of town and immediately races into work to deal with the demands of his own colleagues, other Fairfax papers and news agencies around the world.

"It was a bit busy," Malthus says with his usual sense of understatement. "I didn't really have time or need to coordinate anyone. The photographers just got out there and did what needed to be done, taking their leads from the reporters."

Graphic artists Mark Cornell and John Harford also arrived to construct an epicentre locater for the web, which is updated with news on the worst-affected areas.

Throughout the morning, Holden is in contact with senior Fairfax colleagues in Wellington, in particular group editor John Crowley. A phone conference is called for midday — after a traumatic, exhausting, yet exhilarating morning, *The Press*'s key reporting staff, along with general manager Andrew Boyle, are discussing the event with the *Sunday Star Times* editor and publisher and key digital staff based in Wellington. They assess what has been done and start looking at the enormous appetite for coverage in the *Star*

Left: Photographer Iain McGregor, left, and videographer Dan Tobin film the damage from the sky. **Right:** The temporary newsroom of *The Press* after their evacuation.

Times and *Sunday News*. With only one reporter in Christchurch, the Sunday papers rely heavily on their colleagues at *The Press*.

A special *Press* edition is considered for Christchurch, but instead they opt for *The Press*'s masthead to appear on their front page of the *Sunday Star Times* in the South Island, so that readers will know their local news team is reporting for them.

The true extent of the damage becomes clear when reporter Giles Brown, photographer

coordinates late-breaking events and support troops like Ben Heather, Jo Gilbert, and David Williams, who follows Prime Minister John Key when he arrives to visit the disaster site with photographer Dean Kozanic.

The adrenaline-fuelled journalists pump out so much copy for the Sundays that much never sees the light of day, gets overtaken by new events or is held for the Monday or Tuesday papers.

As the sun sets over the ravaged city, largely without power or water, a group of drained

At the front door of *The Press* he bumps into freelance photographer Lance Burke who had partied through the night, but stumbled out of an inner-city pub once the shaking stopped, and started shooting. He offers some of the first, most compelling shots of the tragedy to *The Press*, which are quickly uploaded.

McGregor and videographer Tobin take to the skies in a helicopter in the afternoon.

Shane Cowlishaw pulls together a wrap piece from *The Press* conferences updating the infrastructure, van Beynen files a story on the several heritage buildings that were damaged, while Brown tells the Sunday readers about the flooding he witnessed from his helicopter ride.

Deputy chief reporter Warren Gamble comes in to relieve Hayman later in the afternoon and

Press reporters and photographers heads back to their families.

Some do not even comprehend the damage they left behind that morning, but they all know the challenges that await them the next day, trying to tell the story to their own readers on Monday morning.

Left: Reporter David Williams works in the second temporary newsroom at the Novotel adjacent to *The Press* building. **Right:** Sports and business reporters get cosy in their new small work stations in the Novotel.

My Quake Story

Livvie Kingi (5) with her sister Bella (9) show earthquake damage at Porritt Park in Christchurch. Photo: Martin Hunter

 **PMP** PRINT

PMP Print in Christchurch kindly provided financial
support for the printing of this book

A RANDOM HOUSE BOOK published by Random House New Zealand
18 Poland Road, Glenfield, Auckland, New Zealand

For more information about our titles go to www.randomhouse.co.nz

A catalogue record for this book is available from the National Library of New Zealand

Random House New Zealand is part of the Random House Group
New York   London   Sydney   Auckland   Delhi   Johannesburg

First published 2010, reprinted 2010

© 2010 text and images *The Press*

The moral rights of the author have been asserted

ISBN 978 1 86979 509 2

Cover photos: top, Iain McGregor; bottom left to right, Iain McGregor, Iain McGregor, David Hallett
Design: Saskia Nicol
Printed in New Zealand by PMP PRINT